MARY RUTH MARKS
REALTOR ®
"THE DRIVING FORCE IN REAL ESTATE"

MOBILE : 608-513-7490
FAX: 608-441-7077
MMarks@BunburyRealtors.com
www.MaryRuthMarks.com

6180 VERONA ROAD • MADISON WI 53719

The Dogs of Madison

Mary Ruth Marks

Notara Press

Verona, Wisconsin

ISBN: 0-9706447-0-1

Layout by Freestyle Graphic Design, Madison, Wisconsin.
Cover by Silverline Studios, Madison, Wisconsin.
Proofing by Eagle Eye Editing, Madison, Wisconsin.
Printed in Stevens Point, Wisconsin.
Published in Verona, Wisconsin.

Inquiries to the publisher should be addressed to:

Notara Press
Mary Ruth Marks
7732 Riverside Road
Verona, Wisconsin 53593
(608) 845-7490
(608) 848-7490 Fax
mrmarks@tds.net   www.equinebasics.com

This book is dedicated to my wonderful brothers and sisters, my sons Tom and Russell, and my first dog Rusty.

Ever since my Mom and Dad died, we Burke children from Mississippi have gotten together every five years for a family reunion. And such a wonderful family it is. Our roots run deep.

May each of your own families grow as strong together as we have.

Ann Burke Anderson
Charles Russell Burke
Dorothy Burke Hemphill
John Scott Burke
Barbara Burke Stockett

I love you all.

Your baby sister and Mom,

Mary Ruth

So what happens when you are trotting in high heels? Splat! Broken foot. Just think if I'd been cantering—should leave that to horses. Darn heels anyway. What to do now? Can't ride my horses, so write that book.

Madison, Wisconsin is such a dog town. Dog park here, dog park there, annual dog jog, dog day care centers, dogtoberfest, dog cemeteries, grooming places, kennel clubs, cosmetologists, training centers, psychologists—along with the usual veterinary clinics and hospitals.

The dogs in this book are from Madison and the surrounding county, whether by referral or by personal "cool dog" sighting. Many a time I'd pull over when I'd see a really neat dog, and ask the owner if their dog would like to be in a book. Sometimes this was on the way to work; many thanks to my boss, Lee Atterbury, for understanding those unexpected late mornings.

What fun! Meeting fun dog owners, their "cool dogs," and capturing each dog's charisma in *The Dogs of Madison.* From drool and slobber to muddy paws and lots of hair, I've loved every minute of this project.

This book was made possible by the wonderful photos taken by Tom Demergian, my friend and most enthusiastic supporter. Thank you Tom D.

Mary Ruth Marks

Bucky

It's a sad reality that there are people who raise dogs for fighting. Happily, Bucky was one puppy rescued from that life early on.

Now six months old, Bucky visits schools, loves kids and is just an all-around Mr. Nice Guy. His most aggressive pastime is chasing grasshoppers around the yard.

Pit Bull

Shetland Sheepdog

Brecca

Brecca's name comes from the Celtic word for "Spot." You will enjoy a demonstration of the Sheltie's working instincts when you peer over her fence and see her herding the family around the back yard.

Brecca's coloring is known as blue merle.

Dakota

Every day, Dakota settles comfortably into her truck and makes the rounds of the family's construction jobs. A born supervisor, she doesn't care much for work.

Dakota is a naturally dominant type who finds that barking is rarely necessary to get her point across. That was certainly a fine trait in the eyes of the quiet-loving Japanese emperors, whose palaces the Akitas guarded.

Akita

Teddy and **Dominic**

Ted has a certain saintly quality, as do all dogs, showing limitless patience as four-month-old housemate Dom bites him and steals his bones and generally interferes with his pursuit of keeping cool.

Ted and Dom were named after Boston Red Sox baseball greats Ted Williams and Dominic DiMaggio.

Great Pyrenees and Basset Hound

Welsh Springer Spaniel

Madison

Maddie can't talk, but it's usually pretty easy to understand what she wants, especially when it's time for her walk. When you take her for a car ride, it's best to let her drive. Otherwise, she'll sit in the back seat and lick your head.

Maddie is one dog who doesn't mind seeing the vet—she lives with one.

Griffin

Griffin *loves* to eat. Among his favored delicacies are couches, mattresses, pillows, shoes, purses, drywall and decorative lighthouses. And if he doesn't like being locked in a room, he eats his way out.

It's likely that the eating thing is just a phase, but there's no mistaking his one true love: the water of Lake Kegonsa.

Yellow Lab

Neapolitan Mastiff

Franny

When Franny is happy, she lies on her back and wiggles, conjuring up images of a beached whale. And this gentle giant is happy most of the time since she was rescued through the Humane Society.

A bit slow to trust strangers, she has a flawless temperament around other dogs and regularly volunteers her services to test new Humane Society dogs for aggressiveness.

Rosie

Rosie was adopted from the Humane Society ten years ago, and can now usually be seen sunning herself in the driveway in front of her friend's transmission shop.

She has an easy way of endearing herself to people. Her letter carrier and UPS driver always bring her treats.

Rosie has shared her love in nursing homes through the Humane Society's Love-a-Pet program. And her visits to local schools, through Humane Education programs, have helped teach children respect, responsibility, and kindness toward animals.

Yellow Lab Mix

Ivy, Sasda, Brindle, and Pepper

A poet once wrote "All dogs are good, any terrier is better, a Scottish Terrier is best." Well, Scottish pride aside, these four certainly overflow with personality. And no, Scotties are not always black.

These dogs all have proper Scottie names on their fine pedigrees, but you won't find them here as they are so Gaelic as to be unspellable and unpronounceable.

Scottish Terriers

Mixed Breed

Odie

Don't let those eyes fool you. Odie is fifty pounds of bad-to-the-bone Bear Dog. It seems he's had a very high opinion of himself ever since he treed a bear in northern Wisconsin last summer. Of course, the bear was only a few months old, but that's not the point. He was there to defend his family when duty called.

Odie has visited nursing homes and been featured in a TV presentation for the Love-a-Pet program. If you follow the cartoons, you know where he got his name.

Erie

Erie is trained to assist the hearing-impaired. You know, a companion hearing dog gets to go places other dogs can't, like restaurants and office buildings and swank hotels and the capitol building. This can lead to tricky situations.

For instance, a man who works at a meat-packing plant might go to a doctor's office and check in at the reception desk. And there might be a young lady seated at that reception desk with Erie lying under the desk beside her. And Erie might stick his nose out from under the desk and begin sniffing and nuzzling the man's foot because it smells like meat. And the man might not realize that it was Erie that was playing with his foot. And…

Welsh Corgi

English Setter

Millie

A *very* active three-month-old English Setter pup, Millie was really more of an UP-Setter when unexpectedly brought home to the family. She also goes by various aliases such as Silly Millie when acting her age, or Millie Minnow when fishing with the family.

Millie's coloring is known as orange belton.

Bubba

Bubba's family owns a bakery. A doggie bakery. Bubba pitches in as the shop's meeter, greeter and taste tester. This is a tough job, but some dog has to do it. As a puppy, Bubba used to gobble down his treats very quickly. But now he has a more discriminating palate and prefers to carefully chew and savor them.

If you live with a Great Dane, you will need a drool cloth in every room. And when you hear running water, quickly yell "OUTSIDE!"

Great Dane

Snickers

Yes, as a matter of fact Snickers does own the road. At least this small stretch of it in front of his Middleton home. Never mind the fact that his family has spent a lot of money installing a state-of-the-art invisible fence system around his yard. Snickers is dog enough to charge through that barrier and assume his daily post in the middle of the street.

Snickers has been run over three times and is blind in one eye, but he's probably sitting in this same spot right now. You just don't tell Snickers where he can and can't go.

Lhasa Apso

Mastiff

Diesel

Diesel is five months old and already weighs over 100 pounds. He lives in an apartment. He has all the natural energy and curiosity of any puppy. Do you see where this is going?

But this big rig is very sweet and well behaved. His sister appears on the 2001 Purina dog food calendar, but we know that Diesel is far too busy to pose for silly photos.

Rottweiler

Stella

Stella was rescued through the Humane Society from an early life of neglect and abuse. She now lives among the beautiful orchids of her new family's greenhouses.

Stella truly is a "star" in the lives of her friends. Her story is typical of many of the lucky dogs in this book who were rescued through the Humane Society. Given a second chance in a loving home, she has given back that love many times over.

Llewellin Setter

Kyrie

Kyrie's Isthmus personal ad would run like this: spunky, young, domineering, attractive and athletic babe seeks submissive male. Must be athletic. I love to swim, run, snowshoe, eat snow on the run and generally keep my nose to the ground. Can do tricks; what can you do?

In people years, Kyrie was twenty-eight on Memorial Day. No, we're not going to tell you; do your own math.

Speedy and Otis

Speedy and Otis are five-year-old brothers. But as the mirror-image markings on their faces warn, life together is not always harmonious. They have been known to literally fight for attention. Still, the fight is short, they get over it, and they move on. Dogs just tend to be more honest about their feelings than people.

They were born in California, where their parents work herding horses. With no horses to herd, Otis is happy to play with his Frisbee. Speedy, who was born deaf, prefers tennis balls.

Australian Cattle Dogs

Nikita

Nikita has seen the old *Thin Man* movies and mastered all of the movie dog's tricks, and then some. She also enjoys modern entertainment, like professional wrestling. Her controversial "Nikita hold," a double-paw pin move applied to humans as well as Arrow, has been banned in fifteen states.

Nikita was a Breeders Network rescue dog.

Wire Fox Terrier

West Highland White Terrier

Arrow

As a puppy, Arrow hated grooming class—his teacher gave him a D-minus and sent him home. But as a teen, he's now much more concerned about his appearance.

Arrow emits a very mournful howl when he thinks he's been left alone, even getting playmate Nikita to chime in.

Mixed Breed

Atrayu

When we lose a loved one, we lose a piece of ourselves.

Shar Pei

Quepos

"Quepos the Wonder Dog" likes to be in control. If he feels like a walk, he brings his leash and stares at you. If he wants to play with the neighbor dog, he simply walks over and bangs on the door. And of course the ladies can't resist his puppy-soft wrinkly face, particularly when he's cruisin' in the ragtop.

Yes, Quepos' tongue is really purple, but not from eating lollipops—it's a breed trait.

Quepos is named for a port in Costa Rica.

Brittany-Springer Spaniel Mix

Otis

When Otis is not looking for rabbits under the house, he is either playing with his tennis ball, basketball, old underwear or old socks. He loves to go fishing, giving any catch a lick before it's tossed back into the lake.

When the Deerfield police car, fire engine or tornado siren goes off, he howls and puckers his lips like he's kissing someone. Go figure.

Muggsy

Now seven years old, Muggsy still loves to play with "dolly," a stuffed toy her family received as a dog-warming gift from the neighbors. Her other hobbies include watching cars go by and sunning herself.

She does not have a stressful life.

When visiting the local horse stables with the family, she likes to run and play with the other animals, pretending that she's roughing it. But when Muggsy gets home, she retreats to her own bedroom with green and pink pastel pillows and a painting of a peaceful garden over the bed.

Boxer

Muffy

Put a doggie treat on the ground in front of Muffy and she will just stare at it, waiting to hear the magic word "okay." Of course, she doesn't take this to extremes. After staring for an hour or so, she'll wander off and look for a bug to play with.

Keeshond and Samoyed Mix

Lucy

Lucy's Frisbee skills are excellent, although her questionable stamina and limited attention span will probably keep her from becoming a world-class canine athlete.

But you must concede it's darn hard to keep your mind on Frisbee practice when there's tall grass to explore nearby.

Mixed Breed

King Charles Spaniel

Alex

In his misspent youth, Alex was the leader of a ragtag band of Maple Bluff hooligans. He earned this mug shot during an important golf tournament, when he and his conspirators took turns dashing onto the golf course, stealing golfers' balls from the greens, and hiding them in the ditch.

This innocent fun earned him in a ride home in a police car.

The Hooligans—**Sophia, Babette,** and **Chloe**

King Charles Spaniels

Moo Shu Van Gogh

Can you guess how Moo Shu got his name? Hint: it's an ear thing.

Wirehaired Dachshund

Dalmatian

Brittany

So what if stripes and spots don't go together? By hogging the bed, Brittany was able to get her own sofa to sleep on, and she likes it.

Brittany is an effective observer of human behavior. She has learned that if she turns up her nose at the first treat, she'll get a second one also. She's often wondered what would happen if she refused the second treat as well, but hasn't been willing to take that chance…yet.

Jackson

Jackson is sure that readers will remember him from his recent appearance in the Land's End catalog. Of course, when working as a professional model, he prefers his check be made out to Darbywood's Jackson Square.

Having outgrown youthful habits like chasing his tail and eating light bulbs, Coke cans and pillows, this star now enjoys regular grooming, baths and trips to the hairdresser.

Airedale

Brigette

Schnauzers were bred in Germany to catch varmints. They guarded the farmers' barns and went along with them to market to guard the produce wagons while the teams rested and the farmers refreshed themselves at the local inn.

Alert, confident, and obviously very agile, Brigette would be a good choice to guard your groceries while you refresh yourself at the local inn.

Schnauzer

Mixed Breed

Graham Cracker

When Graham sees something in the air, he believes in jumping up and grabbing it in his mouth first, then asking questions later. If it turns out to be food, he'll eat it. If it's not food, or if it's shrimp or fruit or vegetables or vitamins or something else icky, he'll spit it out.

Graham likes to roam the neighborhood, howling at people wearing hats. But he always stays within earshot of home, just in case someone lifts the lid on his barking treat jar.

Australian Blue Heeler and Australian Shepherd Mix

Jenny

Some dogs are just perfect. Adopted as a Humane Society surrender dog, Jenny is gentle and quiet, never sits or chews on the furniture, greets you with a warm smile, and just loves everyone.

But perfection depends on your point of view. If you're a rabbit, for example, you will want to steer well clear of her yard.

Winston

Veterinary experts describe Win as "solid" but not obese. His favorite activity? Pretty much a toss-up between eating and sleeping. However, he does occasionally pitch in at the family's accounting practice, where he has been especially useful during IRS audits.

His family, thinking about having puppies, once took him to the local breeder to meet five females. One look at Winston, and they all high-tailed it to the basement. Their loss. He's a heck of a guy.

Bulldog

Standard Poodle

Moses

We cannot verify his assertion that he's the "fastest dog on four legs," but we agree that Moses is exceptional by most measures.

He has set up a nice little bed for himself near the gas fireplace, using fluffy pillows stolen from the family's sofa. And he'll be happy to go out into the woods with you to help look for birds, but don't expect him to put them in his mouth—those feathers tickle.

Smart, obedient and loyal, Moses insists on helping walk the kids to school every morning.

Pomeranian

Koozie

Koozie is a *boy*, thank you very much. And he views the world from a slightly different level.

He was found abandoned on a sand bar in the Wisconsin River, in very bad shape. Now, he's just very happy to be who he is and where he is.

Wren

In true Newtonian fashion, a Scottish Deerhound at rest will tend to remain at rest until acted upon by an outside force, ideally a piece of cheese waved under the nose.

Where Wren and his two brothers live, the kid has his own fenced-in area—the dogs have the run of the house.

Scottish Deerhound

Bearded Collie

Dickens

If you can't find Dickens lounging on the sofa, go ahead and assume that there's a thunderstorm coming and he's balled up in the safety of his crate. His built-in early-warning systems can detect an approaching storm as far away as the state line. And although he doesn't watch much TV, he's smart enough to know the meaning of those storm warning beeps and that crawling weather advisory on the bottom of the screen.

This is one of the few known photos of Dickens, because he's also afraid of cameras.

Chinese Crested

Beijing

How would you feel if all of your body hair was on your ears and feet? Now don't accuse anyone of giving him some cutesy haircut—that's the way Beijing's supposed to look. And he is *not* a wimp. He will chase chipmunks and mice with the best of them, although in winter he would rather stay inside on his heating pad.

Beijing likes to travel in the car, and the highlight of his rides is always the drive-through car wash, where he chases the brushes back and forth and scratches at the windows until near exhaustion.

Austin

Austin's daily commute to her family's Westport boat restoration business is always full of interesting sights and smells. Ah, there's nothing like the wind in your ears.

We don't know much about her early years in Texas. Austin was picked up as a stray in the city which bears her name.

Mixed Breed

American Pointer

Rory

Rory is afraid of birds.

Jack

Jack supervises a horse farm, herding the animals out into the pastures in the morning and back into the barn in the evening. He also serves as welcome wagon to visitors, thoughtfully offering them such bounty as partially eaten tomatoes fresh from the garden.

But whenever he finds a few free minutes in his schedule, Jack likes to curl up with his blanket and suck on it, putting himself into a trance-like state of contentment.

Doberman

Maddie

Maddie was an abused dog rescued by the Humane Society. She didn't stay there long, though. All she had to do was pick out a friendly lady visitor and lean against her longingly, and she had charmed her way into a happy new home.

This Coonhound is not overly active around the house, although she regularly moves across the living room floor, following a small patch of sunlight as she naps. Maddie loves raw hamburger, particularly when it's in a wrapper on the kitchen counter.

Coonhound

Standard Poodle

Bloosie

Bloosie chews on everything—the floor, plants, shoes, legs, other dogs, you name it.

Only ten weeks old and not really naughty by nature, she'll certainly outgrow this habit with time. But she lives with another very clever Standard Poodle who's likely to teach her new ones.

Old English Sheepdog

Willie

Willie is a playful five-month-old who began life in a litter of sixteen puppies. Bottle-fed for several weeks, he eventually got the hang of eating, and at his current growth rate should weigh about 700 pounds in another couple of months.

He enjoys taking the kids for long walks and generally being a "gentle bear."

Smooth Collie

Davis

Davis' story has a happy ending. He was recently adopted from the Human Society, having been badly abused earlier in his life.

His face now lights up when he sees his friends, and he hears magic in the words "dog park."

Wendi

Depending on their age, people have different mental images of this breed. The older ones recall General Patton's dog, while younger folks think of Spuds McKenzie or P.B. from the movie *Babe*.

Popular culture aside, the Bull Terrier is a breed that combines Dalmatian, Terrier and Bulldog. And while experts disagree about how smart they are, there is no disagreement about their stubbornness. Wendi can easily jump five or six feet when playing, but she will not get into the car unless lifted.

Wendi is a very successful show dog.

English Bull Terrier

Travis

Travis loves toys, especially stuffed toys, which he calls his "babies." Specifically, he loves to find their seam, systematically chew out the stitches, and carefully extract all of the stuffing. When finished, he abandons that baby and moves on to the next one. This is a tedious but important job.

Travis would like you to call him "Big Dog."

Dachshund

Coon

A couch potato at home, Coon beams a laser-like intensity when herding sheep. There's a certain awe and joy in the sight of a dog doing what pure instinct has prepared and dedicated training has perfected.

Coon was born in Scotland with a champion's pedigree and has been one of the most consistent working Border Collies in the United States in the last twenty years. He herds animals in response to multiple whistles and voice commands.

Border Collie

Golden Retrievers

Clio and Kelly

Although Clio and Kelly live in a loving household of four Golden Retrievers, these two have a special bond. Clio is soon to become Madison's first privately funded kidney transplant recipient, and Kelly is to be the donor.

Clio is named for the muse of history.

Reggie

If you've been bred to hunt lions, it's a safe bet that you're a pretty tough doggie—the bullies tend to stay away from one Reginald Von Neubauer. Humans are also inclined to be nice to him. Allergic to wheat, he receives special treats made with rice flour.

Take a close look at Reggie, and you'll see how his breed got its name.

Rhodesian Ridgeback

Monty

There is only one other Swedish Vallhund in the Madison area, and he and Monty like to get together and play once a week. Having nearly disappeared completely, the breed was rescued in the 1940's and there are now about 300 in this country.

Monty likes to dig, but only until he hits dirt. So his lawn is full of bare spots, but no holes.

Swedish Vallhund

Llewellin Setter

Mingus

The splashes of color in Mingus' coat are beautiful, but it's obvious that the practical reason for that color is to provide camouflage while hunting. Mingus' idea of hunting is relatively benign, though, limited to pointing and staring and sniffing and creeping around the yard on his belly until his chest is covered with grass stains.

Mingus also likes to point people during his walks through the WIlly Street neighborhood, which seems to confuse them.

Chyna

Not surprisingly, Chyna is a snow dog, rooting around in drifts and banks until her nose turns pink. In the summertime, she makes do chasing squirrels and moles.

Chyna likes to play an especially fun game with the neighbor lady. By creeping across the lawn on her belly until she's near the fence, and then bounding high in the air, Chyna has learned that she can cause the neighbor lady to bound even higher in the air.

Siberian Husky

Eiger

Eiger gets his name from the mountain in Switzerland. In his younger days, he made a cameo appearance in a television commercial for a local tree farm. After meeting this gentle soul, you would really wonder why he was not given a starring role.

Eiger is a classy dog, and very sociable. He hosts a holiday cookie exchange party which is eagerly anticipated each year by all of the neighborhood dogs.

Bernese Mountain Dog

Gizmo

We're not sure who dubbed Gizmo the "King of Bishop's Bay," but if the shoe fits…

When he's not touring his realm on foot, a golf cart serves as his mobile throne.

Gizmo's name comes from the movie *Gremlins*, but his breed can be traced to more classical origins. Lhasa Apsos were used to guard the temples of Tibet, their excellent bark warning of approaching strangers.

Lhasa Apso

Chihuahua

Einstein

If there's a warm, sunny place in the apartment, Einstein will find it and nap there, to the tune of about twenty hours per day. Tipping the scales at just under four pounds, and eating only one-third cup of food each day, he must conserve his energy.

But when playtime does come, this friendly fellow explodes into action, barking like a giant, jumping three times his height, rolling, spinning and chasing a soccer ball that's as big as he is.

English Cocker Spaniel

Vic Tanney

While all of his littermates have gone on to become champion show dogs, Vic prefers his happy life at home. This amicable fellow has even struck up a playful friendship with the squirrel who lives in the rock wall behind his house.

Vic's an avid sportsman. When the kids play ping pong, he and the family's other Cocker love to help out shagging balls. And when the kids don't feel like playing, the Cockers gladly dump the balls out and have their own game.

Saint Bernard

Sitka

Sitka likes to visit the local fifth grade class with a keg around her neck filled with candy. The fifth graders think Sitka is cool.

She is named for her family's favorite Alaska city.

Black Lab

Winston

The Chamber of Commerce would be glad to know that Winston avails himself of the many recreation opportunities offered by Madison's lakes, including fishing, pleasure boating, and jet skiing.

Each morning, he cruises up one side of the family's pier and down the other, hunting for fish in the shallow water. Fortunately for the fish, Winston is not a graceful diver, so they have plenty of warning that he's coming.

Winston has a self-destructive fascination with fireworks, which he likes to eat while they are lit.

Yorkshire Terrier

Miss Fergie

Fergie doesn't do tricks. If cute isn't enough for some people, too bad.

Loving attention, Fergie can be a team player as well. She proudly wears her Brett Favre jersey on Packer football game days.

Black Lab and Rottweiler Mix

Sasha

Sasha is a pure mix of Black Lab exuberance and Rottweiler bulk. A gift to the author from her son, she loves life on a horse farm, especially going on long carriage rides and playing in the pasture with the foals. Her favorite day of the week is Thursday because that's when the neighbors put out their garbage.

Combining the smallest brain size and largest body mass of any dog on the planet, Sasha also has the largest heart and sweetest eyes. And when she wants to hug, she can lean her head on your chest with the force of a hundred dogs.

Bob

Meet Bob the show dog and comedian.
When he arrived in his new home as a
puppy, Bob was given his very own doggie
bed and told that he could put it anywhere
he wanted. He took it directly to the sofa
and it's been there ever since.

Fox Terriers used to be taken along on fox
hunts, carried on horseback in terrier bags.
Once the hounds had chased the fox to
ground, the terrier was released to
fearlessly follow the fox into its den or
through rocky underground passages.

Smooth Fox Terrier

J.J.

Why J.J.? He was named Jake by a kid named Jason.

J.J. is quite the runner and goes for three- to four-mile runs with his owner five to six times a week around Verona. Very intense personality.

He doesn't hunt, but will point.

Vizsla

Hundi

Hundi's name is as noble as they come—it means "doggie" in German. And for sixteen years she has behaved in an appropriately dignified manner, serving by example as mentor to other dogs and small children in the neighborhood.

Once a frequent overseas traveler, Hundi now spends most of her day curled up on the front porch.

Mixed Breed

Australian Shepherd

Shilling

Shilly embodies one of dogs' most wonderful qualities: she can play all day long with the same toy and absolutely never lose interest in it. She just doesn't understand how people can play with her for just a few minutes and then move on to something else.

Maybe that's why Shilly strikes up a hopeful friendship with every stranger, searching like Diogenes for that elusive perfect playmate.

Giant Schnauzer

Hansel

Hans is very happy with who he is. But he does occasionally daydream about being a kid, because kids get to play with such neat stuff. Happily, the family occasionally takes him along to the local playground to climb, slide, and race through the elevated tubes.

Hans has been trained to drink out of the bathtub faucet so that the family can dry his beard after each drink. He's kind of particular about his beard.

Gunther

"Lock up your food, the law dog's coming in tonight." Gunther works two nights each week at the family law office. He's especially helpful with the custodial duties, making the rounds to clean out uneaten lunch remnants from the waste baskets.

Useful at home as well, he helped raise the family children, teaching them to eat out of his bowl. He also lent himself as a moving support when they were learning to walk, and served as the blank canvas on which they practiced their painting.

Weimaraner

Anatolian Shepherd

Reba

Reba is a country dog, although surprisingly she's a bit on the quiet side. She's a self-starter who created her own position as neighborhood caretaker, covering a three-mile radius daily to make sure that all is well.

A very athletic, dynamic and independent type, Reba shows a marked resistance to taking orders. But she insists that it's not her, but rather her breed, which is just not trainable.

Jay and Charlie

Charlie was named for Humphrey Bogart's character in *The African Queen*. Jay's name is just quick and easy to say, which is helpful when you yell at him to stop rolling in the compost pile.

Both Jay and Charlie are on the small side, even for Miniature Poodles, which is helpful when jumping into the dishwasher to lick the plates. Doggie antics aside, though, these are two unusually well-trained males.

Miniature Red Poodles

Chocolate Lab

Griz

Her once deep chocolate-brown coat has turned mostly gray throughout. Her eyes and ears and legs aren't much good for chasing critters anymore. Between naps, Griz prowls the property restlessly, putting neighborhood birds on notice that she's still around.

The "grande dame" of the Cross Plains countryside, Griz will turn seventeen on her next birthday.

Mahli

Mahli's human parents have six college degrees between them, but it's Mahli who calls the shots. When traveling, she will not go to the bathroom in a strange yard—she gets driven to the nearest dog park.

Quiet and docile, Tibetan Terriers were bred as companion dogs for the monks.

Tibetan Terrier

German Wirehaired Pointer

Greta

Greta has this certain intensity and zest for life.

Scarlet

Also known as the African Barkless Dog, the Basenji is one of the oldest dog breeds. The breed's name means "wild and violent" in Swahili, but we detected no such tendencies in red and white Scarlet, who like most Basenjis is feminine, refined, fastidious, proud, alert and energetic.

It's true that Scarlet doesn't bark, but she has an intriguing repertoire of howls and yodels that seem more human than canine.

Basenji

Jack Russell Terrier

Indy

A good shake is one of the very few things that can divert Indy's attention from her tennis ball.

If you ever see Indy and she's not playing with her tennis ball, she's probably eating or sleeping or whining. And whatever she's doing, you can be sure she's wagging her tail. Even while winning her sit-stay and down-stay obedience classes, her tail never quit moving.

Schipperke

Sail

If Sail needs a nap, it's understandable. A top national show dog as well as a beloved companion, she's just finished her seventh show in eight days. That's part of an annual calendar covering more than fifty shows in five states.

Sail can trace her breed's working origins back to the barges and canals of Belgium, where Schipperkes guarded cargo and ate varmints. The breed's name is from a Flemish word meaning "little captain."

German Shepherd

Zepplin

In spite of his heroic looks, Zepplin's whole life revolves around playing.

Playing in the house.
Playing in the barn.
Playing in the truck.
Playing in the yard.
Playing in the river.
Playing with the horses.

Toy Poodle

Scooter

Can you tell that Scooter is a very joyful and outgoing fellow? He just has to run up, flash a friendly smile and say "hi" to everyone and everything he sees, including the fish in the family pond, the geese on the nearby lake, and the golfers on the nearby golf course.

He likes to sleep on your shoulder, although we do not imagine that he sleeps a whole lot.

Schatze

Appropriately, her name means sweetheart in German. Still, those who know her affectionately call her "beast," as she's not above the occasional doggie caper. Like pressing the door-lock button or garage door opener in the van at the worst possible time. Or eating the groceries on the way home from the store. Or rolling in dead, stinky things.

Schatze is one dog who actually enjoys being dressed up, especially on festive occasions when she dons her hula skirt and lei. It's a real floral lei, since Schatze's family owns a Madison nursery.

Brussels Griffon

Gordon Setter

Maggie

Maggie was accidentally dropped into a pool of water as a puppy. A sympathetic type, she'll bark a friendly warning if she sees you in the swimming pool or bathtub.

Maggie has an affinity for high and dry places.

Cindy and Ajax

Their racing careers now over, these Greyhounds are very content just relaxing around the house, except when Riley comes calling.

When playing indoors, Riley neutralizes the Greyhounds' speed advantage and uses his smaller stature to frustrate the them, taking the ball behind the couch and smiling at them.

Greyhounds

Pug

Riley

It has been said that Pugs are the most human-like dogs.

You'd love Riley anyway.

Riley takes a daily walk with the Greyhounds, walking underneath them to enjoy the shade they provide on hot days.

Acknowledgments

Thank you to equine photographer and friend Les Vance, whose comment "the imperfect video completed is better than the perfect one never done," kept me going through another project and now this one. A heartfelt thanks also goes to my silent mentor Bob Mischka, who encourages me at every turn. To friends like these who say "go for it," I say you're wonderful.

A most special thanks to my best friend Tom Demergian, who offered to take the photos. Yes, they're wonderful. They capture the mood, the character and essence of each dog.

During the many days of traveling to and from owners' homes, parks, farms and events, Tom was there with his camera, ready smile and wit. He used two cameras: a Canon AE-1 and a Hasselblad 500C.

Many thanks to my friend, author Mary Bell. She introduced me to the world of writing and publishing as I'd never known. She also led me to Ray Howe, who became a friend and mentor. He is truly a publishing encyclopedia.

Many thanks to the dog owners who gave so willingly of their time. Every story you told helped make this book a reality.

To Tish Hodges, a fellow carriage driver and judge, who brought me to this book, a most heartfelt thanks.

A special thank you to my dog Sasha, as she was the one who would sit by my side and keep me going till all hours of the day and night. Her chest-crushing hugs and reverse

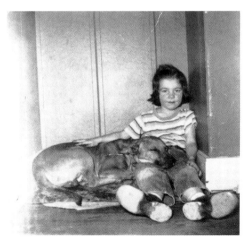

Mary Ruth and Rusty, 1953

hugs under the chin were diversions much welcomed. She is not the smartest dog I've ever owned, but she's the sweetest and most understanding. I still wish she wouldn't drool water on the toilet seat.

Thanks to friends who saw what I wanted to do and helped with an encouraging word, action or thought: Randy and Diane Wixson, Kim Dearth, Deb Davis and Marti Coursin. Many of you helped me through my broken foot: Deb Halsted, Julie Selzer, Jean Raspel, Dave Tarr and Judy Dvorak. Others put up with me and my crazy dog: thanks go to Denny Achenbach and Tom Demergian.

A big thank you to my at-work supporters. You listened, laughed, and encouraged me at every turn: Abby, LynnZ, Linda, Mary Ann, Joni, Anita, Kristi, Kerri, Jason, Alex, Mike, Ray, Lee and Swing.

Thanks guys,

Mary Ruth